THE KINGFISHER
First
Picture Atlas

Written by Deborah Chancellor

Illustrated by Anthony Lewis

KINGFISHER

KINGFISHER

Kingfisher Publications Plc
New Penderel House
283–288 High Holborn
London WC1V 7HZ

www.kingfisherpub.com

Author: Deborah Chancellor
Senior editor: Belinda Weber
Art director: Mike Davis
Consultant: Keith Lye
DTP Manager: Nicky Studdart
Senior production controller: Lindsey Scott
Picture research manager: Cee Weston-Baker
Proof-reader: Sheila Clewley
Cover design: Mike Davis, Jane Tassie

Illustrations by Anthony Lewis

First published by Kingfisher
Publications Plc 2005

10 9 8 7 6 5 4 3 2

2TR/0506/SHENS/CLSN(CLSN)/158MA/CTP

Copyright © Kingfisher
Publications Plc 2005

A CIP catalogue record for this book
is available from the British Library.

ISBN-13: 978 0 7534 1300 5
ISBN-10: 0 7534 1300 0

Printed in Taiwan

Contents

CREDITS
The Publisher would like to thank the following for permission
to reproduce their material. Every care has been taken to trace copyright
holders. However, if there have been unintentional omissions or failure to
trace copyright holders, we apologise and will, if informed, endeavour to
make corrections in any future edition.

2 NASA; 7 Corbis/Galen Rowell; 8 Corbis/Yann Arthus-Bertrand; 13
Photolibrary/Walter Bibikow; 15 Alamy/Robert Harding Picture Library;
16 Alamy/Bob Turner; 19 Alamy/ Robert Harding Picture Library; 20
Alamy/Imagestate; 22 Alamy/Andre Jenny; 24 Alamy/Mervyn Rees; 27
Corbis/ Reuters; 28 Getty/311214-001; 30 Corbis/Arko Datta/Reuters;
32 Alamy/SC Photos; 35 Alamy/Worldwide Pic Lib; 37 Photolibrary/John
Downer; 38 Corbis/Yann Arthus-Bertrand; 41 Alamy/Robert Harding
Picture Library; 42 Rex; 43 Getty/Stone; 45 Alamy/Nordicphotos

About the earth

The earth is a planet in space. It is shaped like a ball and is covered with land and sea. Photographs can show us what the earth looks like. Maps help us understand more about the world.

Countries of the world

A country (such as Italy, map above) is a part of the world with its own people and laws. There are over 200 countries in the world. The number changes if countries break up or join together in new ways.

Continents

A continent is a huge mass of land. Some continents, such as South America (map above), contain many different countries. On maps of continents, lines are drawn to show the borders between countries. You cannot see these lines on a photograph, because they are not really there.

What is a map?

A map is a picture of the earth that shows natural and man-made features. A globe is a kind of map that is in the shape of a ball, just like the earth itself. We cannot see the whole world at once on a globe. If we want to do this, we need to look at a flat map.

Making a map

To make a flat map, the globe is split into segments, and 'peeled' like an orange.

The segments are then placed side by side.

These segments are used to create a flat map (see the map of the world on page 10).

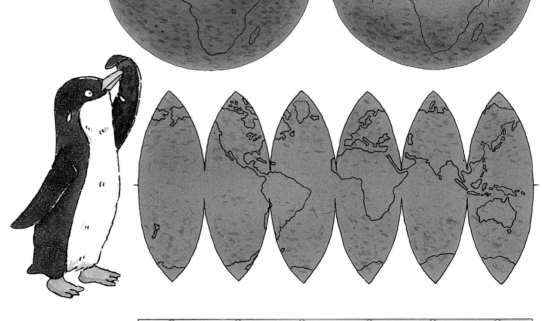

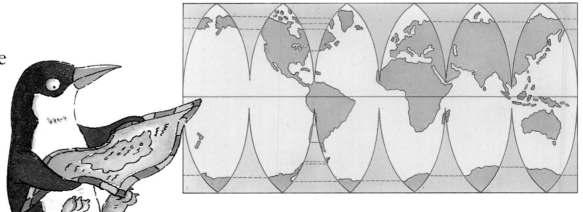

6

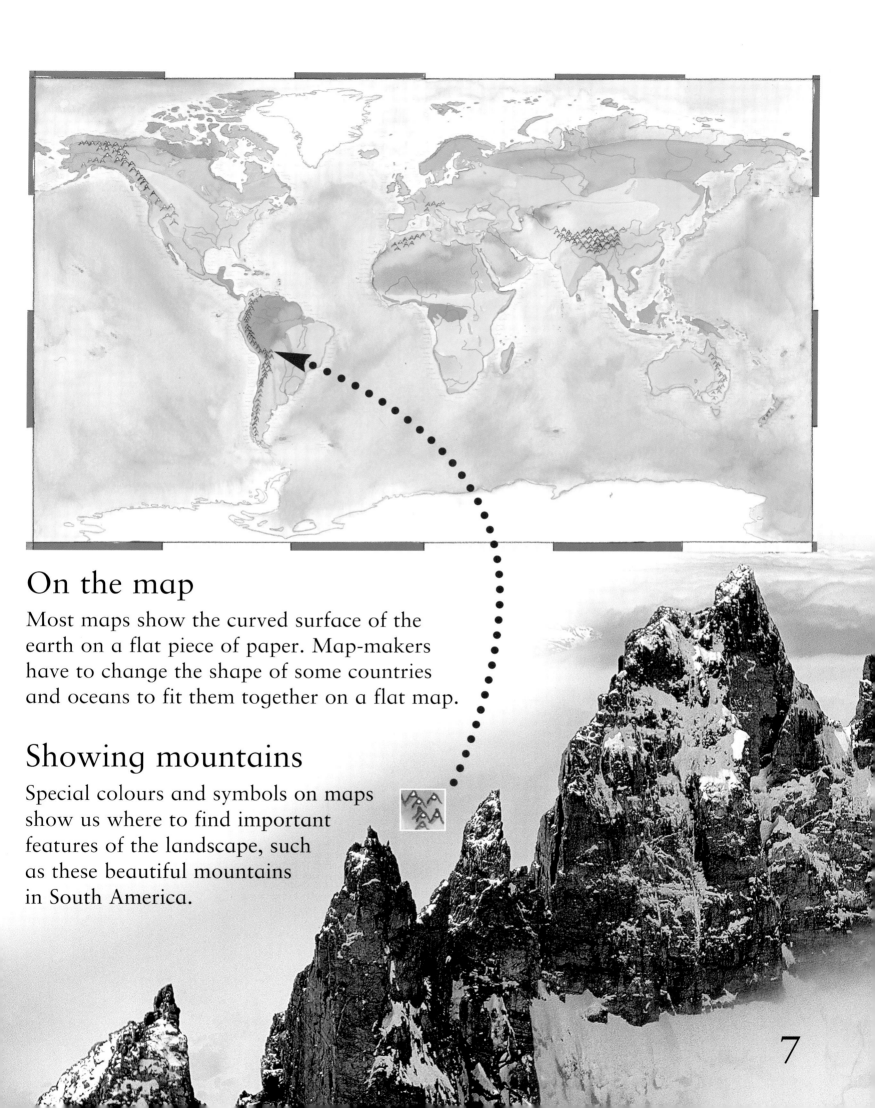

On the map

Most maps show the curved surface of the earth on a flat piece of paper. Map-makers have to change the shape of some countries and oceans to fit them together on a flat map.

Showing mountains

Special colours and symbols on maps show us where to find important features of the landscape, such as these beautiful mountains in South America.

Using an atlas

An atlas is a book of maps. To use an atlas, you need to understand how maps work. Maps are much smaller than the places they show. They have lots of information in a very small space.

Pictures show industries, animals or landmarks.

Grid band 'C'

A small world map shows you where to find the countries shown on the main map.

Grid band '2'

A grid helps you find places on the map. Here, Alice Springs is in square C2. You can find this by tracing your finger down from the letter C band and across from the number 2 band.

In this atlas, a story box picks out an interesting fact.

Darwin

Seahorse

Gulf of Carpentaria

Abbriginal cave painting

NORTHERN TERRITORY

Great Sandy Desert

A U S T R A L I

TROPIC OF CAPRICORN

Mining

Gibson Desert

Alice Springs

Simpson Desert

WESTERN AUSTRALIA

SOUTH AUSTRALIA

Kangaroo

Lake Eyre

Great Victoria Desert

The Ghan

Perth

Farming

Great Australian Bight

Adelaide

Great white shark

Uluru is a sandstone monolith rising high above the desert in Australia's Northern Territory. It is the largest rock of its kind in the world.

Look for the star ✦

38

A   B   C

A   B   C

8

Map key

Colours, lines and symbols on maps stand for many different things. These details are explained in a key to the map. In this atlas, the key helps you find cities, borders and rivers. It also shows what the colours on the map mean.

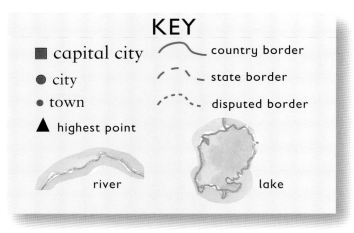

KEY

■ capital city — country border
● city ⌐ ¬ state border
• town ⌐ ¬ disputed border
▲ highest point

river   lake

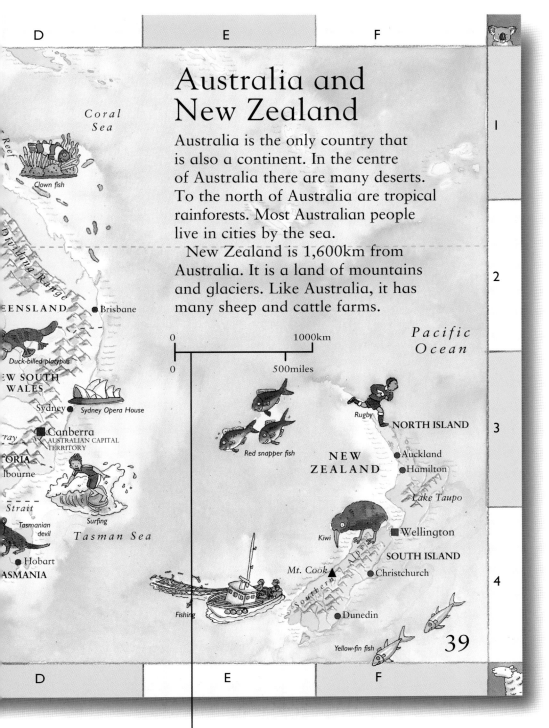

Australia and New Zealand

Australia is the only country that is also a continent. In the centre of Australia there are many deserts. To the north of Australia are tropical rainforests. Most Australian people live in cities by the sea.

New Zealand is 1,600km from Australia. It is a land of mountains and glaciers. Like Australia, it has many sheep and cattle farms.

Coral Sea

Clown fish

Duck-billed platypus

Brisbane

EENSLAND

NEW SOUTH WALES

Sydney • Sydney Opera House

■ Canberra
AUSTRALIAN CAPITAL TERRITORY

ORIA

Ibourne

Surfing

Tasmanian devil

Tasman Sea

• Hobart

ASMANIA

0   1000km
0   500miles

Red snapper fish

Rugby

NORTH ISLAND

NEW ZEALAND

• Auckland
• Hamilton

Lake Taupo

Kiwi

■ Wellington

SOUTH ISLAND

Mt. Cook ▲   • Christchurch

Fishing

• Dunedin

Yellow-fin fish

Pacific Ocean

39

A scale bar helps you understand how big areas are on the map.

Desert Dry areas with sand and rocks

Dry grassland Flat, grassy plains with only a few trees

Temperate grassland Flat, grassy plains with some trees

Forest Areas with lots of trees

Mountains Tall hills and rugged landscape

Tundra Flat area near Arctic with frozen ground and no trees

Ice and snow Places where ice and snow cover the ground

Seas and oceans Salty water that covers much of the earth

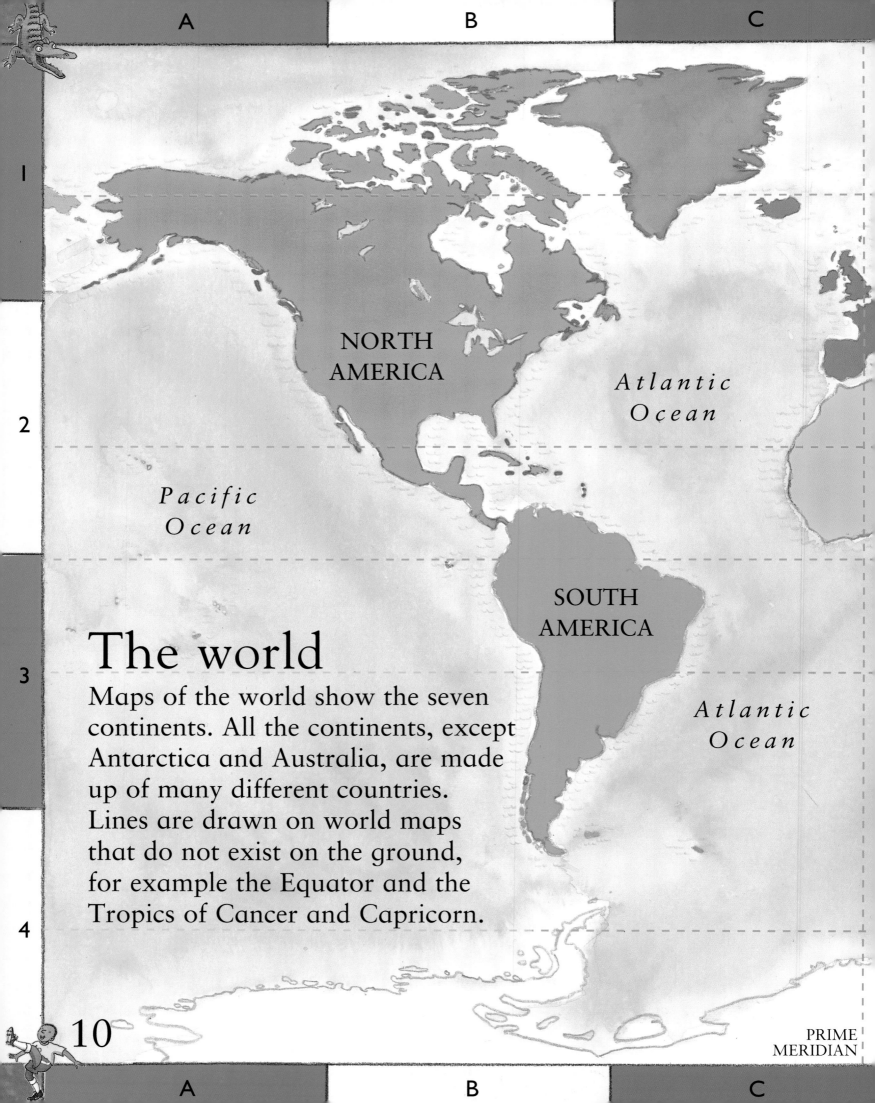

NORTH
AMERICA

*Atlantic
Ocean*

*Pacific
Ocean*

SOUTH
AMERICA

The world

Maps of the world show the seven
continents. All the continents, except
Antarctica and Australia, are made
up of many different countries.
Lines are drawn on world maps
that do not exist on the ground,
for example the Equator and the
Tropics of Cancer and Capricorn.

*Atlantic
Ocean*

10

PRIME
MERIDIAN

ARCTIC CIRCLE

1

Arctic Ocean

ASIA

EUROPE

TROPIC OF CANCER

2

Pacific Ocean

AFRICA

EQUATOR

Indian Ocean

TROPIC OF CAPRICORN

3

AUSTRALIA

Southern Ocean

ANTARCTIC CIRCLE

4

ANTARCTICA

11

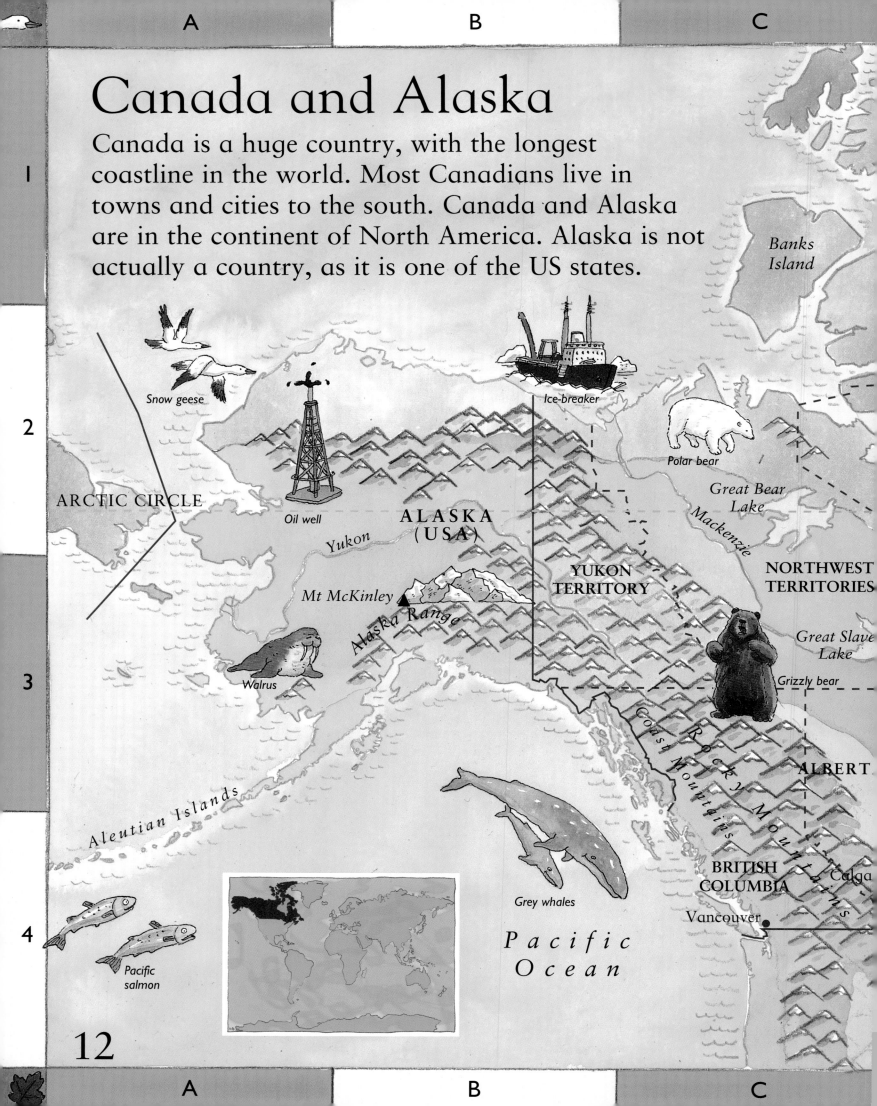

Canada and Alaska

Canada is a huge country, with the longest coastline in the world. Most Canadians live in towns and cities to the south. Canada and Alaska are in the continent of North America. Alaska is not actually a country, as it is one of the US states.

Banks Island

Snow geese

Ice-breaker

Polar bear

Great Bear Lake

Oil well

ARCTIC CIRCLE

Yukon

ALASKA (USA)

Mackenzie

YUKON TERRITORY

NORTHWEST TERRITORIES

Mt McKinley

Alaska Range

Great Slave Lake

Walrus

Grizzly bear

Aleutian Islands

Coast Mountains

Rocky Mountains

ALBERT

Grey whales

BRITISH COLUMBIA

Calga

Vancouver

Pacific salmon

Pacific Ocean

Queen Elizabeth Islands

Ellesmere
Island

Devon
Island

Victoria
Island

Québec City is the only walled city in North America. It was founded in 1608, and is almost 400 years old.

Look for the star ✸

Baffin
Island

N U N A V U T

Reindeer

Inuit

ARCTIC CIRCLE

Lake
Athabasca

H u d s o n
B a y

Iceberg

MANITOBA

A t l a n t i c
O c e a n

C A N A D A

SASKATCHEWAN

Lake
Winnipeg

Timber industry

Skier

QUEBEC

NEWFOUNDLAND
AND LABRADOR

Arable farming

ONTARIO

Lake
Superior

Toronto's
CN Tower

Industry

St Lawrence

NEW
BRUNSWICK

0   1000km

Lake
Huron

Montreal

PRINCE
EDWARD
ISLAND

0   500miles

Lake
Erie

Ottawa

Lake Ontario

NOVA SCOTIA

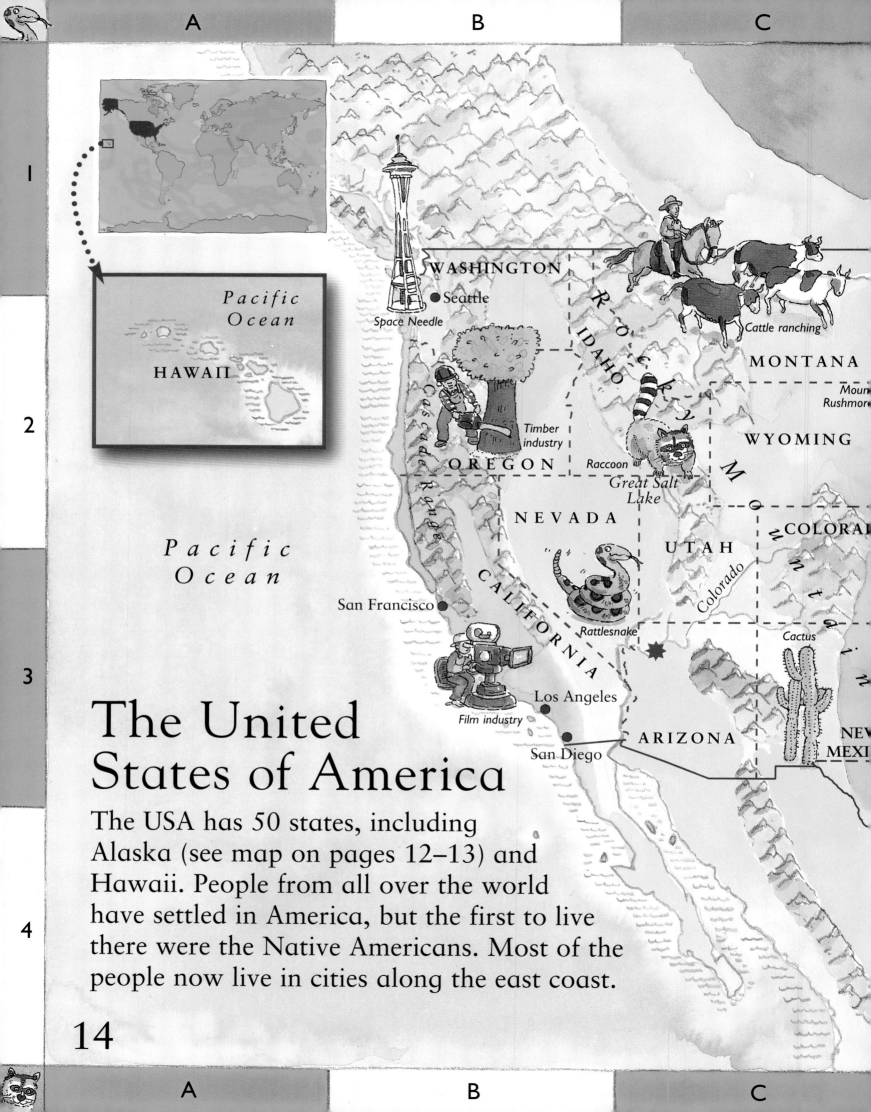

Pacific Ocean

HAWAII

Pacific Ocean

WASHINGTON
● Seattle
Space Needle

Cascade Range

Timber industry

OREGON

NEVADA

CALIFORNIA

San Francisco ●

Film industry

Los Angeles ●

San Diego ●

ROCKY

IDAHO

Raccoon

Great Salt Lake

UTAH

Rattlesnake

Colorado

Cactus

ARIZONA

MONTANA

Mount Rushmore

WYOMING

COLORADO

Mountains

NEW MEXICO

Cattle ranching

The United States of America

The USA has 50 states, including
Alaska (see map on pages 12–13) and
Hawaii. People from all over the world
have settled in America, but the first to live
there were the Native Americans. Most of the
people now live in cities along the east coast.

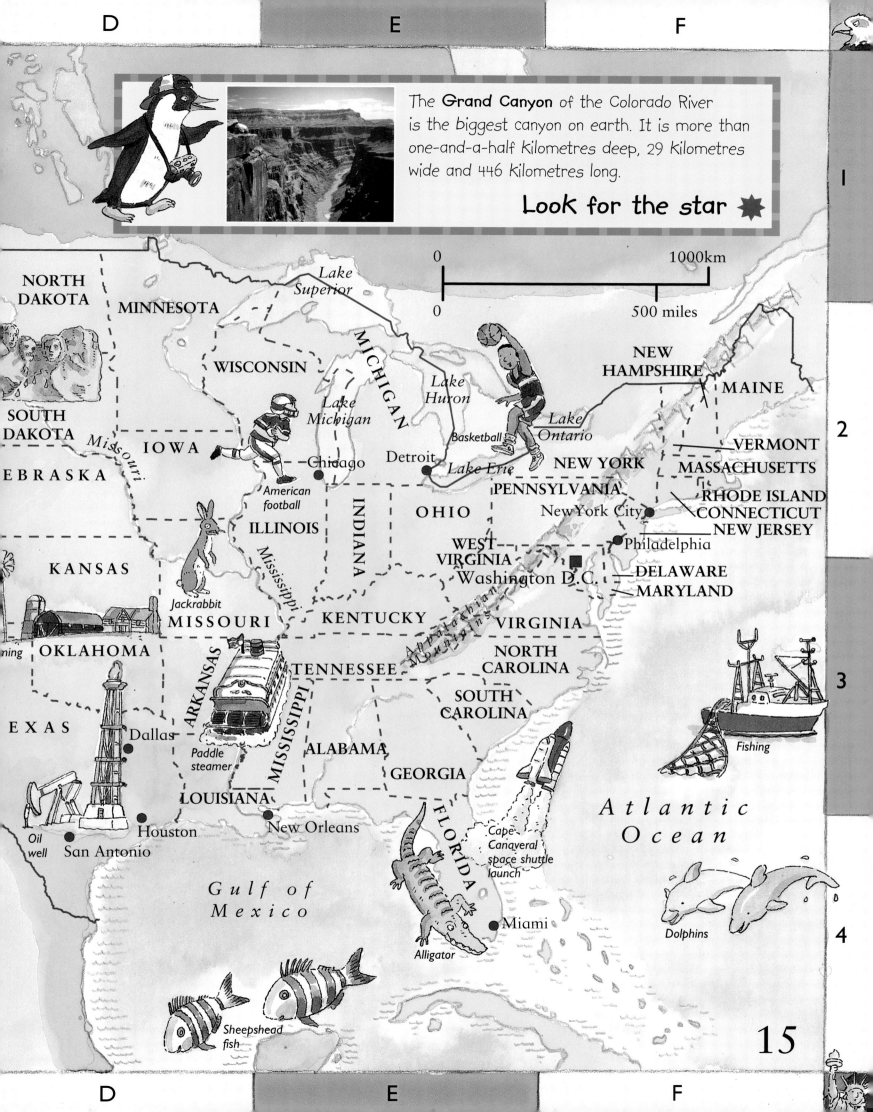

D   **E**   **F**

The **Grand Canyon** of the Colorado River is the biggest canyon on earth. It is more than one-and-a-half kilometres deep, 29 kilometres wide and 446 kilometres long.

Look for the star ✦

0   1000km

0   500 miles

NORTH DAKOTA

MINNESOTA

Lake Superior

NEW HAMPSHIRE

MAINE

SOUTH DAKOTA

WISCONSIN

MICHIGAN

Lake Huron

Lake Michigan

Missouri

IOWA

American football

Lake Ontario

Basketball

VERMONT

EBRASKA

Chicago

Detroit

Lake Erie

NEW YORK

PENNSYLVANIA

MASSACHUSETTS

RHODE ISLAND

CONNECTICUT

NEW JERSEY

ILLINOIS

INDIANA

OHIO

New York City

KANSAS

Mississippi

Jackrabbit

WEST VIRGINIA

Washington D.C.

Philadelphia

DELAWARE

MARYLAND

MISSOURI

KENTUCKY

Appalachian Mountains

VIRGINIA

ning

OKLAHOMA

ARKANSAS

TENNESSEE

NORTH CAROLINA

SOUTH CAROLINA

Fishing

EXAS

Dallas

Paddle steamer

MISSISSIPPI

ALABAMA

GEORGIA

Atlantic Ocean

Oil well

Houston

San Antonio

LOUISIANA

New Orleans

FLORIDA

Cape Canaveral space shuttle launch

Gulf of Mexico

Alligator

Miami

Dolphins

Sheepshead fish

15

The **Trinidad Carnival** is one of the biggest in the Caribbean. Bands, including steel bands, play music and people dance in the streets. The steel drum was invented in Trinidad.

Look for the star ✦

Rio Grande

MEXICO

Gulf of California

West Sierra Madre

East Sierra Madre

Flounder

Gulf of Mexico

Maize farming

Oil rig

Yucatán Peninsula

■ Mexico City

Mayan temple

BELI

Belmopan ■

Bananas

Fishing

Pacific Ocean

Tourism

GUATEMALA

Guatemala City ■

San Salvador ■

EL SALVADOR

Managua ■

COSTA RIC

0   1000km

0   500miles

Sea turtle

Mexico, Central America and the Caribbean

Mexico, Central America and the Caribbean islands are in the continent of North America. Mexico is the largest country in the region. The islands of the Caribbean are countries too. More than half of all Caribbean people live in Cuba and the Dominican Republic.

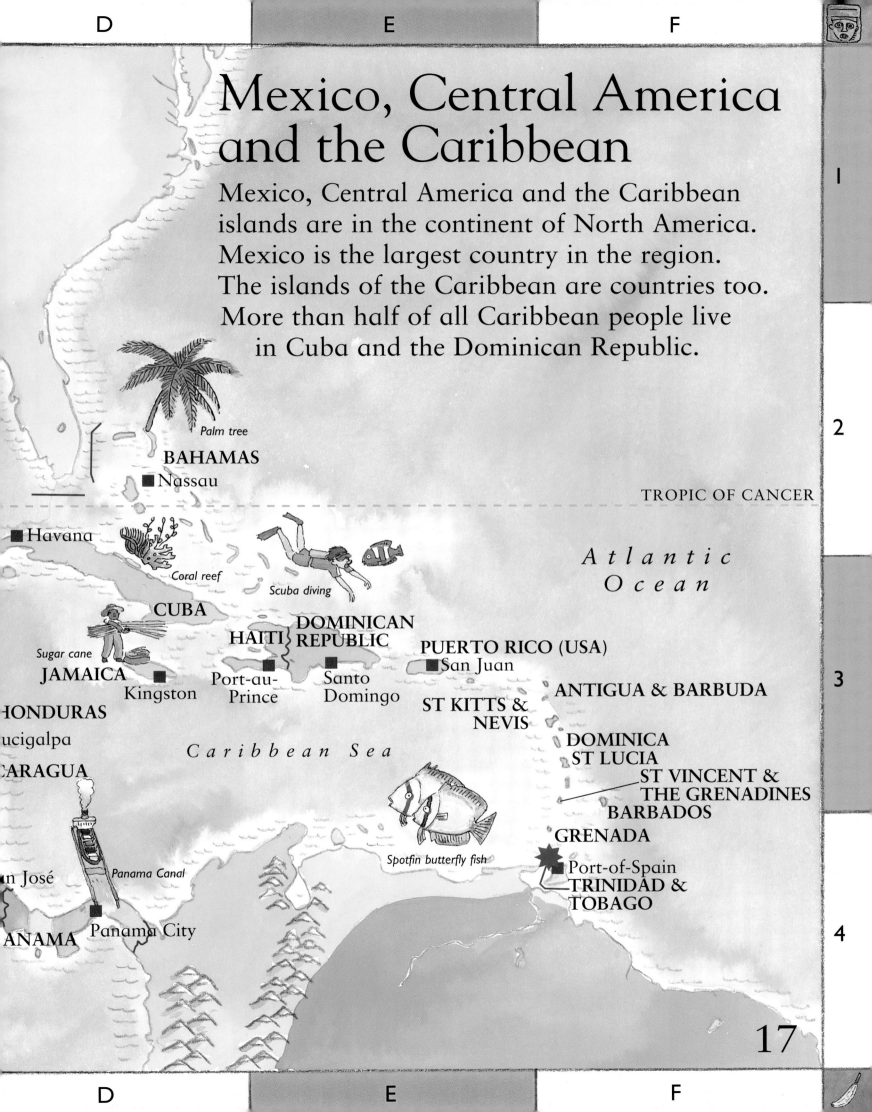

Palm tree

BAHAMAS

■ Nassau

TROPIC OF CANCER

■ Havana

Coral reef

Scuba diving

Atlantic Ocean

CUBA

Sugar cane

DOMINICAN REPUBLIC

HAITI

PUERTO RICO (USA)

■ San Juan

JAMAICA

■ Kingston

Port-au-Prince

Santo Domingo

ANTIGUA & BARBUDA

ST KITTS & NEVIS

HONDURAS

ucigalpa

Caribbean Sea

DOMINICA
ST LUCIA

CARAGUA

ST VINCENT & THE GRENADINES

BARBADOS

GRENADA

Spotfin butterfly fish

n José

Panama Canal

Port-of-Spain
TRINIDAD & TOBAGO

ANAMA   Panama City

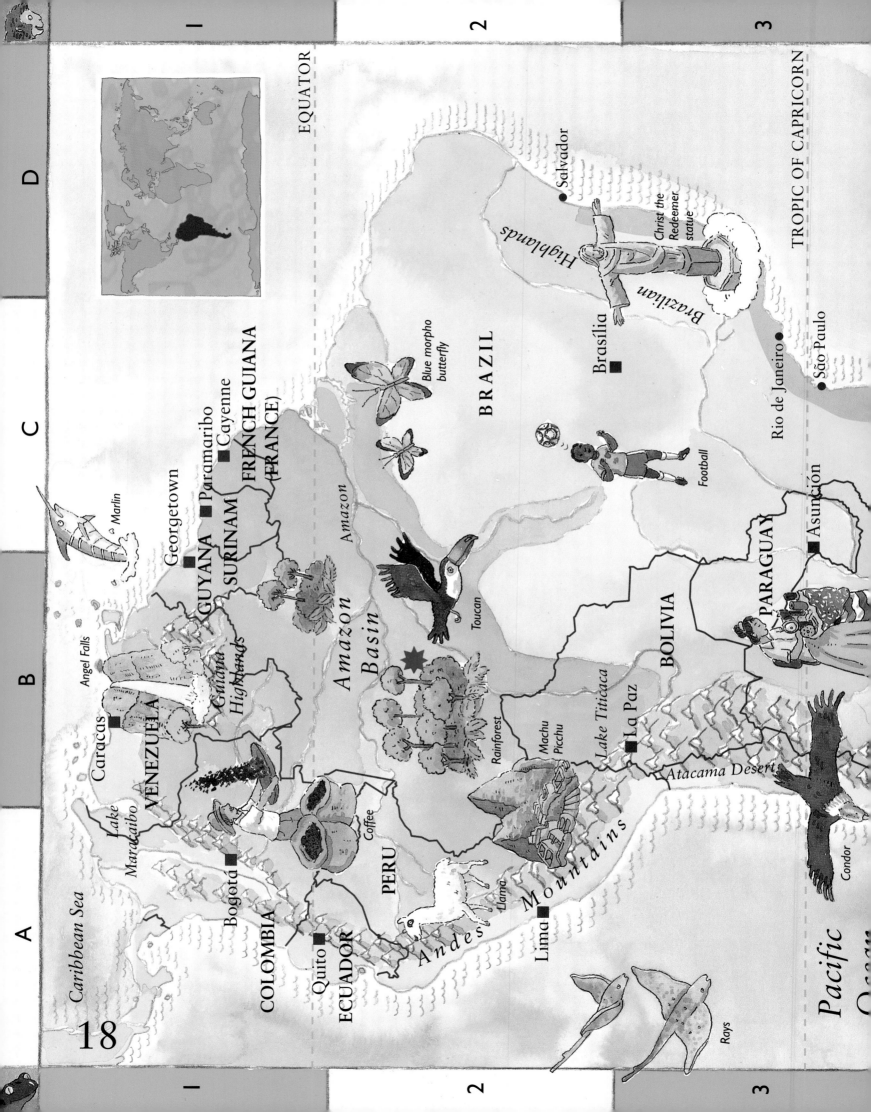

EQUATOR

TROPIC OF CAPRICORN

18

D   C   B   A

1   2   3

Caribbean Sea

Lake Maracaibo

Angel Falls

Caracas

VENEZUELA

Bogotá

COLOMBIA

Quito

ECUADOR

Guiana Highlands

Georgetown

GUYANA

Paramaribo

SURINAM

Cayenne

FRENCH GUIANA (FRANCE)

Marlin

Amazon

Amazon Basin

Coffee

PERU

Lima

Andes Mountains

Llama

Machu Picchu

Rainforest

Lake Titicaca

La Paz

BOLIVIA

Atacama Desert

Toucan

Blue morpho butterfly

BRAZIL

Brazilian Highlands

Brasília

Salvador

Christ the Redeemer statue

Rio de Janeiro

São Paulo

Football

PARAGUAY

Asunción

Pacific Ocean

Condor

Rays

South America

South America is a continent of extremes. Tall, snowy mountains lie to the west, while the steamy Amazon rainforest covers a huge area to the north. The southern tip of the continent is very dry and freezing cold.

Aeroplane

URUGUAY
■Montevideo

Santé Fé●
Paraná

■Buenos
Aires

ARGENTINA

Sheep farming

Oil rig

FALKLAND
ISLANDS (UK)
■Stanley

Mt Aconcagua
Santiago■

Andes Mountains

Grapes

Concepción●
CHILE

Patagonia

Cape Horn

Sardines

Fishing

The Amazon rainforest contains about half of all the animal and plant species in the world. Many are still waiting to be discovered.

⭐ **Look for the star**

0	1000km
0	500miles

19

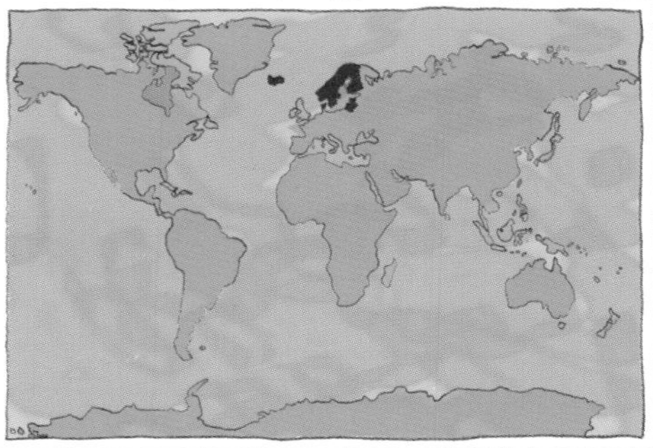

1

Northern Europe

Forests, lakes and mountains cover large parts of northern Europe. The countries Norway, Sweden and Denmark make up a region called Scandinavia. To the east lies Finland. South of the Baltic Sea are the small countries of Estonia, Latvia and Lithuania.

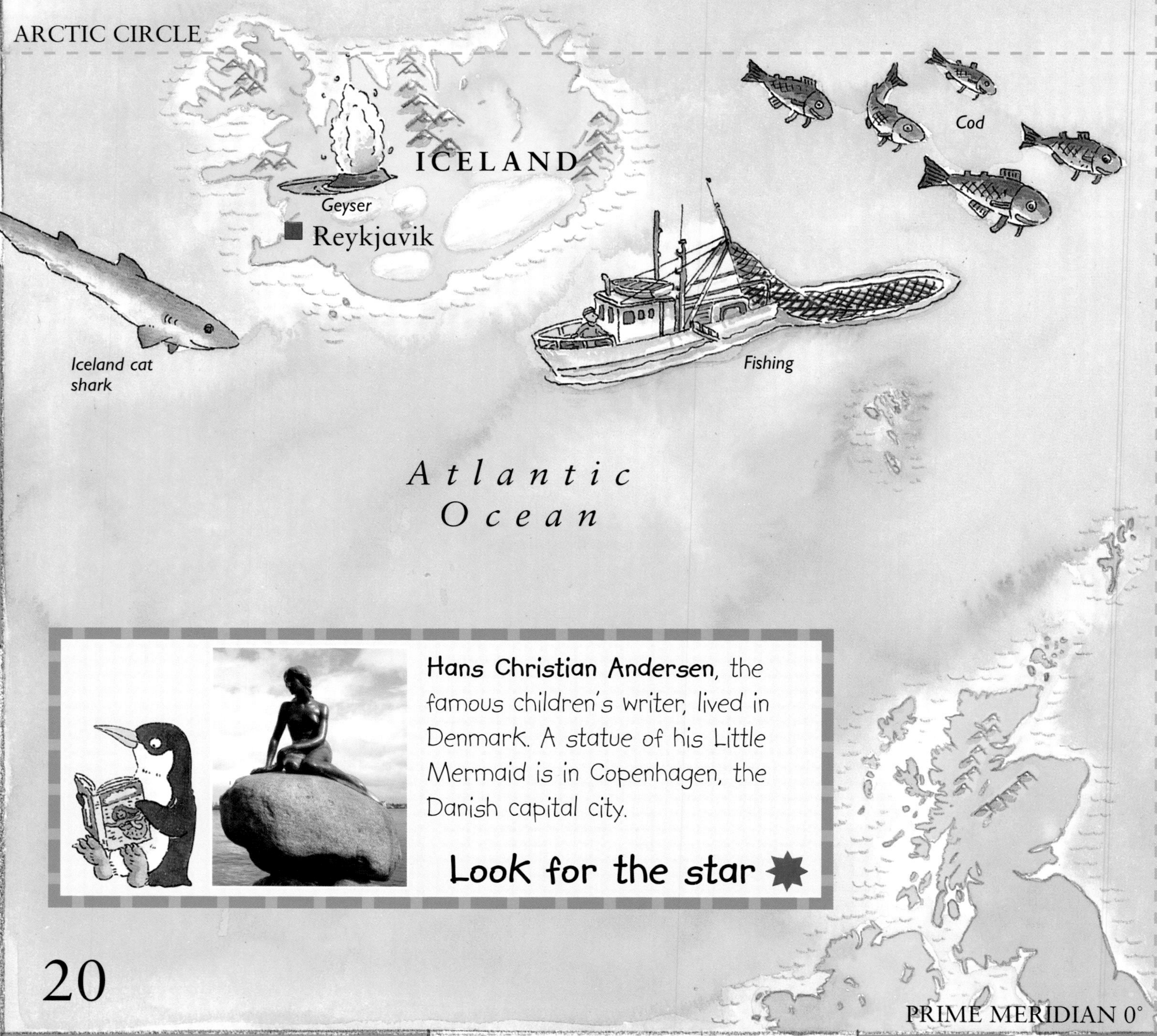

ARCTIC CIRCLE

2

ICELAND

Geyser

Reykjavik

Cod

Iceland cat shark

Fishing

3

A t l a n t i c
O c e a n

Nor
Sea

Hans Christian Andersen, the famous children's writer, lived in Denmark. A statue of his Little Mermaid is in Copenhagen, the Danish capital city.

Look for the star ✸

4

PRIME MERIDIAN 0°

0   400km

0   200miles

● Hammerfest

L a p l a n d

Fishing

● Kiruna

Arctic fox

Fjord

ARCTIC CIRCLE

Norwegian Sea

Reindeer and Sami

Pine forest

FINLAND

Oil rig

● Trondheim

SWEDEN

● Oulu

Lake Oulujärvi

Paper mills

L a k e   r e g i o n

Pine forest

Gulf of Bothnia

NORWAY

Bergen

● Oslo ■

Åland

● Helsinki ■

Gulf of Finland

Industry

Stockholm ■

Baltic Sea

■ Tallinn

Lake Vänern

ESTONIA

Lake Vättern

Gotland

LATVIA

● Gôteborg

■ Ríga

Pig farming

Cattle farming

DENMARK

■ Copenhagen

Lego

LITHUANIA

Vilnius ■

21

Western Europe

Much of the land in western Europe is used for farming. Industries, such as car factories, are also important. Some cities are very old, and attract many tourists. Countries around the Mediterranean Sea are very hot in summer.

France's most famous landmark, the **Eiffel Tower**, sways up to 12cm from side to side in high winds.

Look for the star

Atlantic Ocean

Baltic Sea

Car industry

Tulips

Windmill

Oil rig

North Sea

NETHERLANDS

Cod

Puffin

SCOTLAND

● Edinburgh

UNITED KINGDOM

NORTHERN IRELAND

● Belfast

■ Dublin

Computers

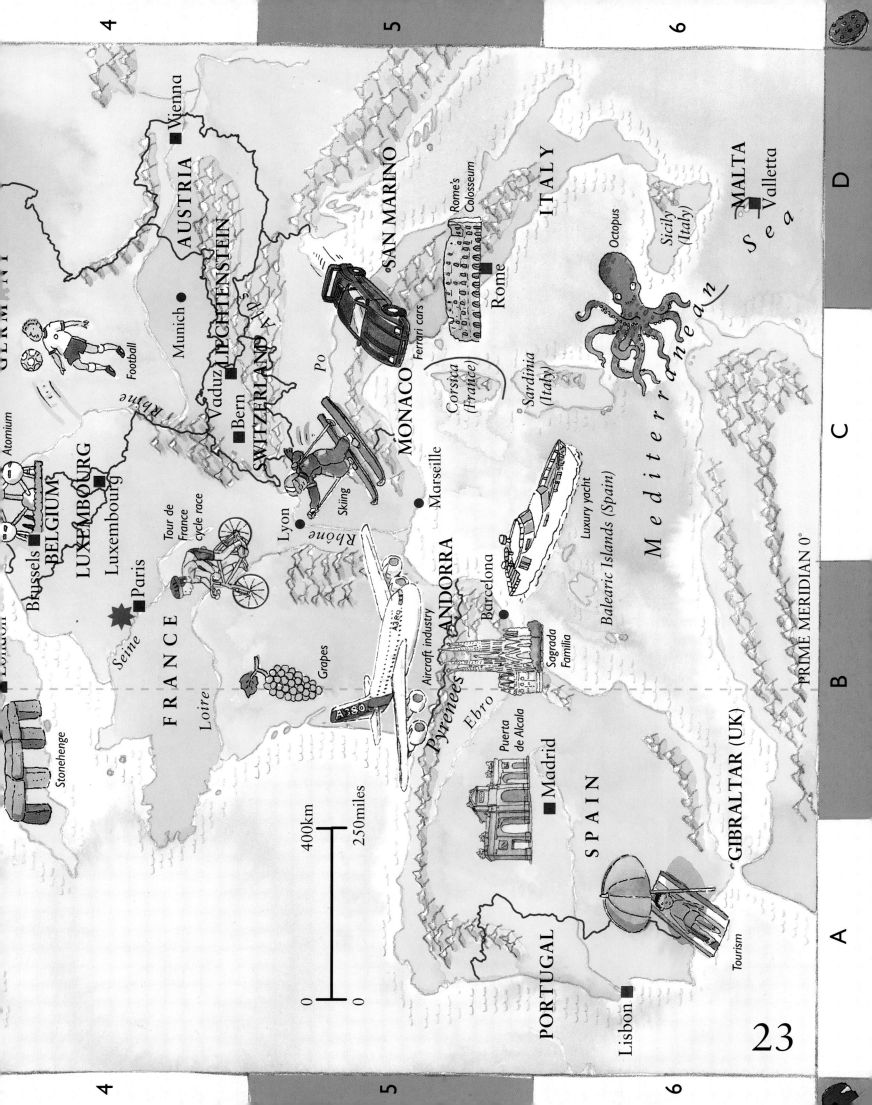

GERMANY

Vienna
■ AUSTRIA

Munich ●

Vaduz ■ LIECHTENSTEIN

Bern ■

SWITZERLAND Alps

Football

Atomium

Brussels
■ BELGIUM

LUXEMBOURG

Luxembourg
■

Paris
■

F R A N C E

Loire

Grapes

Tour de
France
cycle race

Rhône

Seine

Lyon ●

Skiing

Po

SAN MARINO

Rome's
Colosseum

Rome
■

I T A L Y

Ferrari cars

MONACO

Corsica
(France)

Marseille ●

Sardinia
(Italy)

Octopus

Sicily
(Italy)

MALTA
■
Valletta

M e d i t e r r a n e a n   S e a

ANDORRA

Pyrenees

Barcelona ●

Sagrada
Familia

Luxury yacht

Balearic Islands (Spain)

Ebro

Aircraft industry

A380

Stonehenge

London

Puerta
de Alcala

Madrid
■

S P A I N

GIBRALTAR (UK)

PRIME MERIDIAN 0°

PORTUGAL

Lisbon
■

Tourism

400km

0

2.50miles

0

A   B   C   D

4

5

6

23

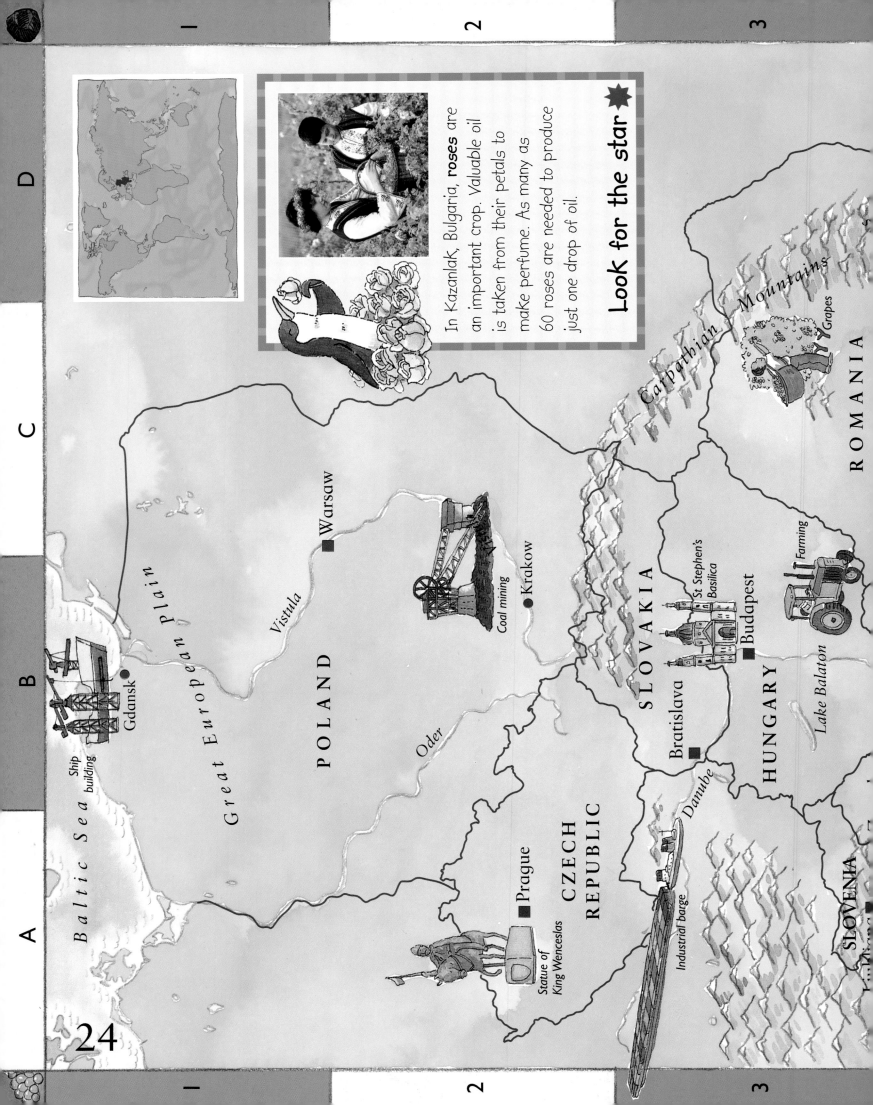

D **C** **B** **A**

1 2 3

Baltic Sea

Ship building

● Gdansk

Great European Plain

POLAND

Vistula

■ Warsaw

Oder

Coal mining

● Krakow

Statue of King Wenceslas

■ Prague

CZECH REPUBLIC

Danube

Industrial barge

SLOVAKIA

Bratislava ■

St Stephen's Basilica

■ Budapest

HUNGARY

Farming

Lake Balaton

SLOVENIA

Carpathian Mountains

Grapes

ROMANIA

In Kazanlak, Bulgaria, **roses** are an important crop. Valuable oil is taken from their petals to make perfume. As many as 60 roses are needed to produce just one drop of oil.

★ Look for the star

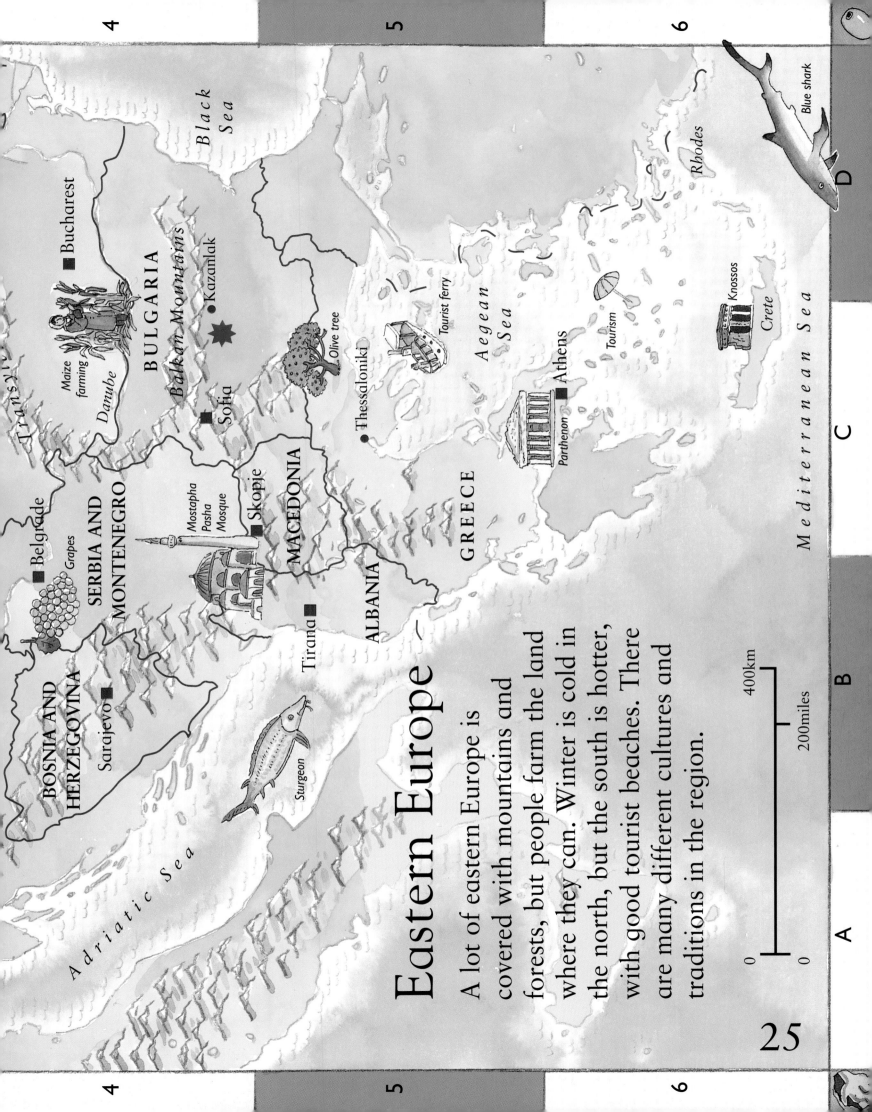

Eastern Europe

A lot of eastern Europe is covered with mountains and forests, but people farm the land where they can. Winter is cold in the north, but the south is hotter, with good tourist beaches. There are many different cultures and traditions in the region.

0 | 200miles
0 | 400km

BOSNIA AND HERZEGOVINA
■ Sarajevo

Grapes

SERBIA AND MONTENEGRO
■ Belgrade

Mostapha Pasha Mosque

■ Skopje
MACEDONIA

■ Tirana
ALBANIA

Sturgeon

Adriatic Sea

Transyl...

■ Bucharest

Maize farming

Danube

BULGARIA
Balkan Mountains

■ Sofia

● Kazanlak

Black Sea

Olive tree

● Thessaloniki

GREECE

Tourist ferry

Aegean Sea

■ Athens
Parthenon

Tourism

Knossos

Crete

Rhodes

Mediterranean Sea

Blue shark

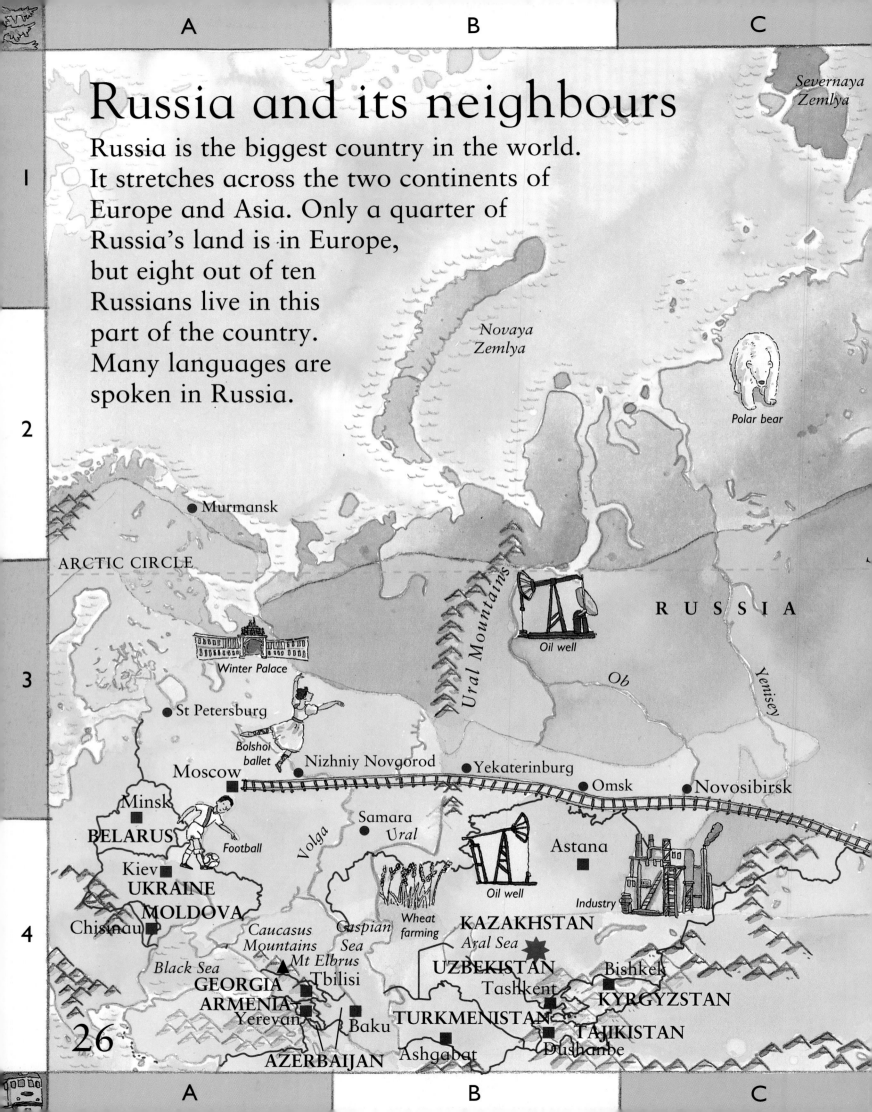

Russia and its neighbours

Russia is the biggest country in the world. It stretches across the two continents of Europe and Asia. Only a quarter of Russia's land is in Europe, but eight out of ten Russians live in this part of the country. Many languages are spoken in Russia.

Severnaya Zemlya

Novaya Zemlya

Polar bear

Murmansk

ARCTIC CIRCLE

R U S S I A

Winter Palace

Ural Mountains

Oil well

Ob

Yenisey

St Petersburg

Bolshoi ballet

Nizhniy Novgorod

Moscow

Yekaterinburg

Omsk

Novosibirsk

Minsk

Football

Volga

Samara

Ural

Astana

BELARUS

Kiev

UKRAINE

MOLDOVA

Chisinau

Caucasus Mountains

Caspian Sea

Wheat farming

Oil well

KAZAKHSTAN

Aral Sea

Industry

Black Sea

Mt Elbrus

UZBEKISTAN

Bishkek

GEORGIA

Tbilisi

Tashkent

KYRGYZSTAN

ARMENIA

Yerevan

Baku

TURKMENISTAN

TAJIKISTAN

26

AZERBAIJAN

Ashgabat

Dushanbe

The **Baikonur cosmodrome** in Kazakhstan is the world's biggest space launching station. Many rockets are launched from there.

Look for the star ✴

Taymyr Peninsula

New Siberian Islands

Walrus

Polar cod

Pine forest

Lena

S i b e r i a

East Siberian Uplands

Diamond mining

● Yakutsk

Gold mining

Lake Baikal

Trans-Siberian Railway

Amur

Tiger

Fishing

Kamchatka Peninsula

Sea of Okhotsk

Seal

Pacific Ocean

● Vladivostok

Black Sea

● Istanbul

■ Ankara

TURKEY

● Izmir

Tourism

Sheep farming

Euphr...

■ Nicosia

CYPRUS

SYRIA

*M e d i t e r r a n e a n
S e a*

Beirut ■
LEBANON

■ Damascus

ISRAEL

Jerusalem ■ ■ Amman

JORDAN

Bedouin nomad

Red Sea

● Medin...

Southwestern Asia

Many countries in southwestern Asia have hot, sandy deserts. The region is rich in oil and natural gas. Crops can grow only where there is water, in the lands near the Mediterranean, Caspian and Black seas. Eastern Turkey and northern Iran have mountains, plains and grasslands, which are cold in winter.

The Great Mosque

Mecca ●

*Ocellat...
wasp f...*

Few people live in the hot deserts of southwestern Asia, but some **Bedouin** nomads wander around its edges. Their camels travel up to 160 kilometres a day.

Look for the star ✦

1

2

3

4

0   800km

0   500miles

1

Caspian Sea

Tabriz

Mosul

Oil rig

Mashhad

Tigris

Tehran

Onager

Baghdad

I R A N

IRAQ

Esfahan

Zagros Mountain

2

Basra

KUWAIT

Kuwait City

The Gulf

Oil refinery

Oil well

BAHRAIN

SAUDI ARABIA

Manama

OMAN

Oil well

QATAR

Doha

Riyadh

Abu Dhabi

3

U. A. E.

Muscat

TROPIC OF CANCER

Arabian Desert

OMAN

Dhow

*Empty Quarter
(Rub al Khali)*

Arabian Sea

Arabian oryx

YEMEN

Sana

Orange-spotted trevally

4

Dates

Gulf of Aden

Aden

29

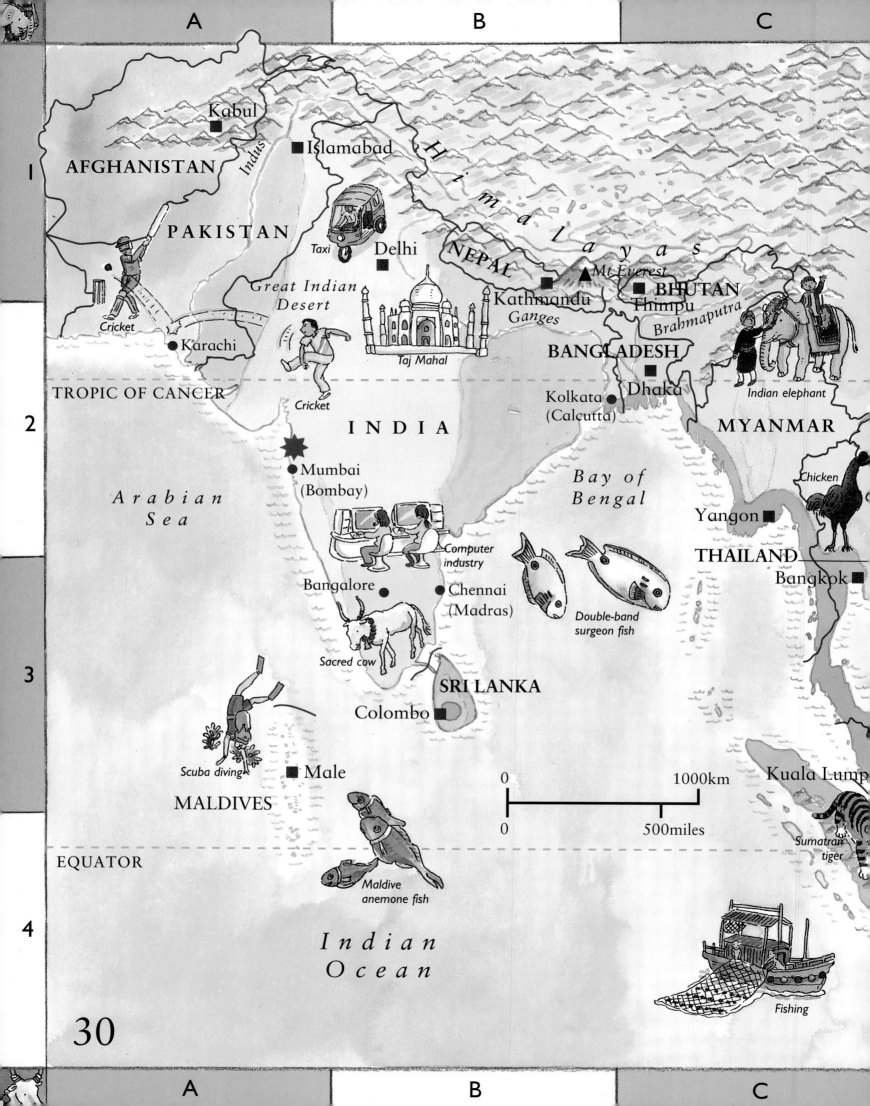

1

Kabul

Islamabad

AFGHANISTAN

Indus

PAKISTAN

Taxi

Delhi

Himalayas

NEPAL

▲ *Mt Everest*

Kathmandu

BHUTAN

Thimpu

Cricket

Great Indian Desert

Taj Mahal

Ganges

Brahmaputra

BANGLADESH

Indian elephant

Karachi

TROPIC OF CANCER

2

Cricket

INDIA

Kolkata (Calcutta)

Dhaka

MYANMAR

Arabian Sea

★ Mumbai (Bombay)

Bay of Bengal

Chicken

Yangon

Computer industry

Bangalore

Chennai (Madras)

Double-band surgeon fish

THAILAND

Bangkok

Sacred cow

3

SRI LANKA

Colombo

Scuba diving

Male

Kuala Lump

MALDIVES

Sumatran tiger

EQUATOR

Maldive anemone fish

4

Indian Ocean

0   1000km

0   500miles

Fishing

30

Southern and southeastern Asia

The countries of this region are near the
equator, so the weather is very hot. Dusty
plains stretch across India. Thick rainforests
grow in Malaysia and Indonesia. Most
people farm in small villages, or work
in big cities. A long mountain range
called the Himalayas lies to the north.

VIETNAM
■ Hanoi
OS
ntiane

*South China
Sea*

Mekong

Basket boat

MBODIA

Rice

■ Manila

Phnom
Penh

PHILIPPINES

Oil rig

BRUNEI
Begawan Seri

ALAYSIA

SINGAPORE
ngapore

Orang utan

I N D O N E S I A

■Jakarta

■Dili
EAST TIMOR

Rainforest

The world's biggest movie
industry, **Bollywood**, is
based in Mumbai
(Bombay), India. About
800 new films are made
here every year.

Look for
the star ✴

31

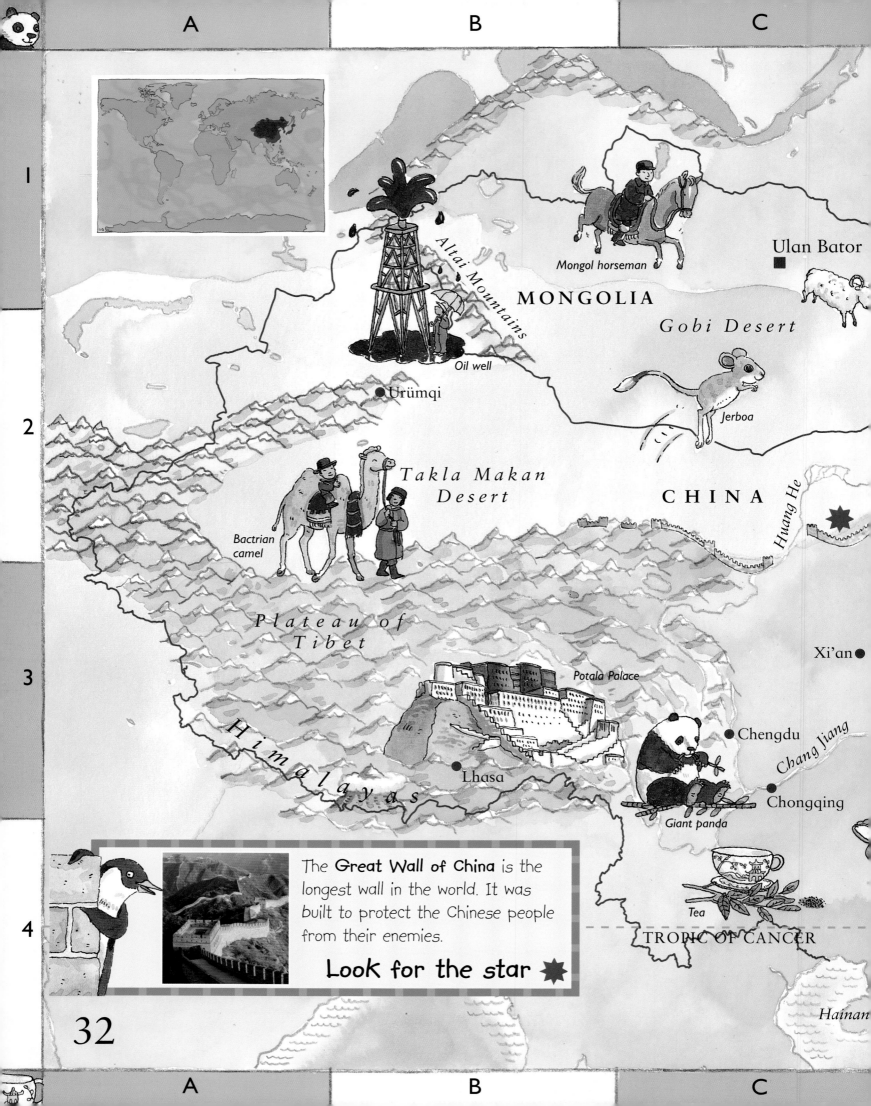

A   B   C

I

2

3

4

Altai Mountains

Oil well

Urümqi

Takla Makan Desert

Bactrian camel

Plateau of Tibet

Himalayas

Potala Palace

Lhasa

MONGOLIA

Mongol horseman

Ulan Bator

Gobi Desert

Jerboa

CHINA

Huang He

Xi'an

Chengdu

Chang Jiang

Chongqing

Giant panda

Tea

TROPIC OF CANCER

Hainan

The **Great Wall of China** is the longest wall in the world. It was built to protect the Chinese people from their enemies.

Look for the star ✦

A   B   C

0   1000km

0   500miles

1

Great Khingan Range

Sheep farming

Harbin

Industry

Hokkaido

2

The Forbidden City

Shenyang

Honshu

Sea of Japan

Squid

Bullet train

Beijing

Tianjin

NORTH KOREA

Pyongyang

Seoul

Bulguksa temple

JAPAN

Terracotta warriors

SOUTH KOREA

Himeji Castle

Mt Fuji

Tokyo

Nagoya

Osaka

3

Chinese junk

Wuhan

Shanghai

East China Sea

Shikoku

Kyushu

China and Japan

More people live in China than anywhere else on earth. Most settle in the east, where they can farm the land or work in cities. To the north is Mongolia, and to the east are Korea, Taiwan and Japan. Japan is made up of many islands. Most Japanese people live on the four main islands, Hokkaido, Honshu, Shikoku and Kyushu, in very crowded cities.

Rice

Taipei

TAIWAN

4

Guangzhou

Hong Kong

South China Sea

33

A

B

C

Atlantic Ocean

PRIME MERIDIAN 0°

Mediterranean

Algiers

Tunis

1

Rabat

Atlas Mountains

TUNISIA

Citrus fruits

Tripoli

Oil well

MOROCCO

ALGERIA

LIBYA

Laâyoune

Berber and camels

WESTERN
SAHARA

S a h a r a

2

*Ahaggar
Mountains*

MAURITANIA

*Tibesti
Mountains*

Nouakchott

NIGER

C

Niger

Cattle

Hippopotamus

SENEGAL

Lake Chad

Dakar

BURKINA

Niamey

GAMBIA

FASO

N'Djamena

3

Banjul

Bamako

Bissau

Peanuts

Ouagadougou

NIGERIA

GUINEA-
BISSAU

GUINEA

Niger

Conakry

Diamonds

IVORY

Abuja

Freetown

COAST

SIERRA LEONE

GHANA

TOGO

BENIN

Monrovia

Yamoussoukro

Oil well

LIBERIA

Accra

Lomé

Porto Novo

*Street
market*

4

EQUATOR

0   1000km

34

0   500miles

Fishing

PRIME MERIDIAN 0°

Northern Africa

The Sahara is the world's biggest desert. It stretches across the whole of northern Africa. Most people live south of the Sahara or near the coast. The world's longest river, the Nile, flows from central Africa, through Egypt to the Mediterranean Sea.

TROPIC OF CANCER

EGYPT

Tutankhamun's funerary mask

Scorpion

Cairo

Lake Nasser

Red Sea

ASIA

Nile

Cotton plant

Crocodile

ERITREA

Khartoum

Asmara

SUDAN

Ethiopian Highlands

DJIBOUTI

Addis Ababa

ETHIOPIA

Starry triggerfish

SOMALIA

Mogadishu

The **pyramids**, near Cairo in Egypt, were built over 4,000 years ago. They are the largest stone buildings in the world.

Look for the star ✦

Indian Ocean

35

Southern Africa

Countries on the east coast of Africa, such as Kenya, are famous for the wildlife of the flat grasslands. Lions, elephants and giraffes all live in the savannah. To the west of Africa, the River Congo runs through thick rainforest. The huge Kalahari Desert is at the heart of southern Africa.

SEYCHELLES
Victoria

EQUATOR

Freight ship

Long distance runner

Great Rift Valley

UGANDA
Kampala

KENYA
Nairobi

Lake Victoria

RWANDA
Kigali

BURUNDI
Bujumbura

TANZANIA
Dodoma

Mt Kilimanjaro

Lake Tanganyika

Great Rift Valley

Copper mine

African elephant

Chimpanzee

CENTRAL AFRICAN REPUBLIC

Congo

DEMOCRATIC REPUBLIC OF CONGO

Bangui

Football

CAMEROON
Yaoundé

CONGO
Brazzaville

Kinshasa

Libreville

GABON

ANGOLA
Luanda

Malabo

EQUATORIAL GUINEA

São Tomé

SÃO TOMÉ & PRÍNCIPE

Maize

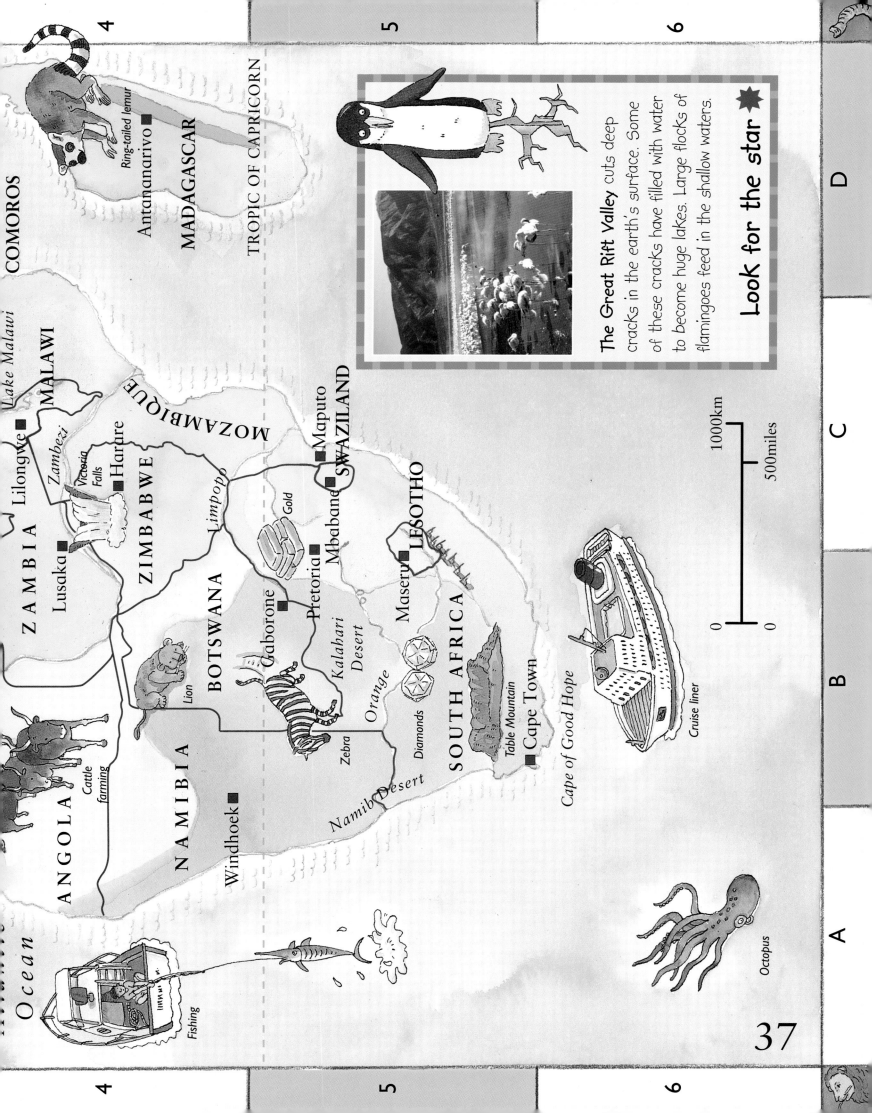

Indian Ocean

COMOROS

MADAGASCAR

Antananarivo ■

Ring-tailed lemur ■

TROPIC OF CAPRICORN

Lake Malawi

MALAWI

Lilongwe ■

ZAMBIA

Lusaka ■

Zambezi

Victoria Falls

Harare ■

ZIMBABWE

MOZAMBIQUE

Maputo ■

SWAZILAND

Mbabane ■

Limpopo

Gold

Pretoria ■

Gaborone ■

BOTSWANA

LESOTHO

Maseru ■

Kalahari Desert

Orange

Diamonds

Zebra

Lion

NAMIBIA

ANGOLA

Cattle farming

Windhoek ■

Namib Desert

SOUTH AFRICA

Table Mountain

Cape Town ■

Cape of Good Hope

Cruise liner

Fishing

Octopus

The **Great Rift Valley** cuts deep cracks in the earth's surface. Some of these cracks have filled with water to become huge lakes. Large flocks of flamingoes feed in the shallow waters.

★ Look for the star

0   500miles
0   1000km

4

5

6

A   B   C   D

37

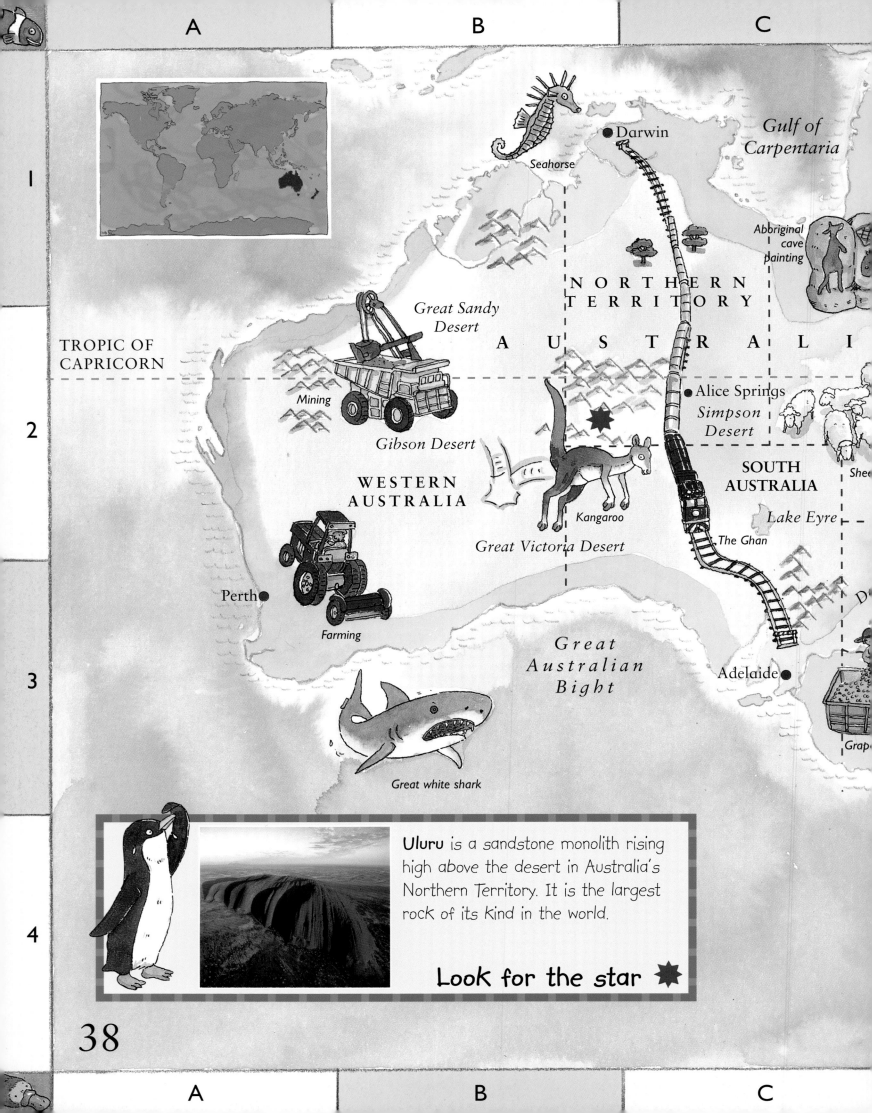

1

Gulf of Carpentaria

• Darwin

Seahorse

Abriginal cave painting

N O R T H E R N
T E R R I T O R Y

A U S T R A L I

TROPIC OF
CAPRICORN

Great Sandy Desert

Mining

2

Gibson Desert

• Alice Springs
Simpson Desert

SOUTH
AUSTRALIA

Shee

WESTERN
AUSTRALIA

Kangaroo

Lake Eyre

The Ghan

Great Victoria Desert

Perth •

Farming

3

Great Australian Bight

Adelaide •

D

Grap

Great white shark

4

Uluru is a sandstone monolith rising high above the desert in Australia's Northern Territory. It is the largest rock of its kind in the world.

Look for the star ✦

Australia and New Zealand

Australia is the only country that is also a continent. In the centre of Australia there are many deserts. To the north are tropical rainforests. Most Australian people live in cities by the sea.

New Zealand is 1,600km from Australia. It is a land of mountains and glaciers. Like Australia, it has many sheep and cattle farms.

Coral Sea

Clown fish

Barrier Reef

Great Dividing Range

JEENSLAND

● Brisbane

Duck-billed platypus

NEW SOUTH WALES

Sydney ●

Sydney Opera House

urray

■ Canberra
AUSTRALIAN CAPITAL TERRITORY

TORIA

Melbourne ●

Surfing

ss Strait

Tasmanian devil

Tasman Sea

● Hobart

TASMANIA

1000km

500miles

Pacific Ocean

Red snapper fish

Rugby

NORTH ISLAND

NEW ZEALAND

● Auckland

● Hamilton

Lake Taupo

Kiwi

■ Wellington

Southern Alps

SOUTH ISLAND

Mt Cook ▲

● Christchurch

Fishing

● Dunedin

Yellow-fin fish

39

I

North Pacific Ocean

TROPIC OF CANCER

NORTHERN MARIANA ISLANDS (USA)

WAKE ISLAND (USA)

GUAM (USA)

Anchovies

MARSHALL ISLANDS

Aeroplane

M i c r o n e s i a

Majuro

2

■ Koror

Palikir ■

PALAU

FEDERATED STATES OF MICRONESIA

M e l a n e s i a

EQUATOR

■ Yaren

Fishing

Tarawa ■

NAURU

KIRIBATI

Rainforest

▲ *Mt Wilhelm*

PAPUA NEW GUINEA

SOLOMON ISLANDS

Funafuti ■

TOKELAU (NZ)

■ Honiara

TUVALU

AMERICAN SAMOA (U

■ Port Moresby

Coral Sea

VANUATU

WALLIS AND FUTUNA IS. (FRANCE)

SAMOA

3

■ Apia

Coral reef

Port-Vila ■

Rugby

■ Suva

Tourism

NIUE (NZ)

COO ISLANI (NZ)

NEW CALEDONIA (FRANCE)

FIJI ISLANDS

TONGA

TROPIC OF CAPRICORN

Bananas

Nuku'alofa ■

KERMADEC ISLANDS (NZ)

S o u t

4

Tiger shark

40

The Pacific Islands

There are thousands of islands in the Pacific Ocean. All these islands, with Australia, New Zealand and Papua New Guinea, make up a region called Oceania. Many Pacific islanders live in communities that have little contact with the rest of the world. Some of their traditions have not changed for centuries.

Over 1,000 years ago, settlers on Easter Island carved these huge **heads** out of volcanic rock. The statues may represent the island's great chiefs.

Look for the star ✴

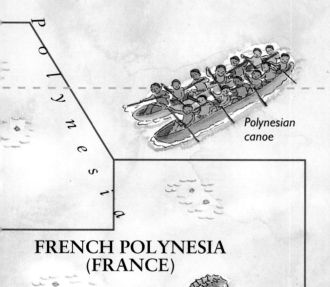

Polynesian canoe

FRENCH POLYNESIA (FRANCE)

Tahiti

Long-nosed seahorses

Cruise liner

GALÁPAGOS ISLANDS (ECUADOR)

Sea turtle

PITCAIRN ISLANDS (UK)

TROPIC OF CAPRICORN

✴ **EASTER ISLAND (CHILE)**

P a c i f i c   O c e a n

0   1000km

0   500miles

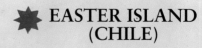

Humpback whale

41

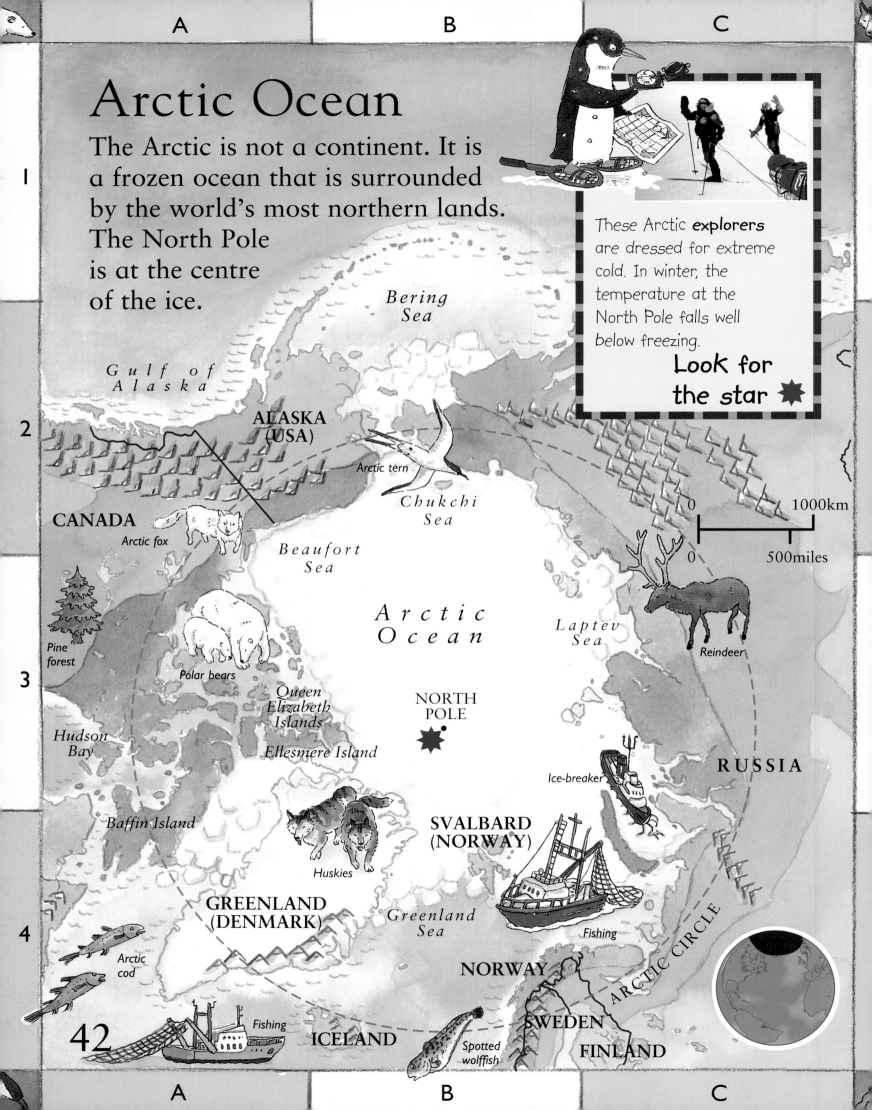

Arctic Ocean

The Arctic is not a continent. It is a frozen ocean that is surrounded by the world's most northern lands. The North Pole is at the centre of the ice.

These Arctic **explorers** are dressed for extreme cold. In winter, the temperature at the North Pole falls well below freezing.

Look for the star ✴

1

2

3

4

Bering Sea

Gulf of Alaska

ALASKA (USA)

Arctic tern

Chukchi Sea

CANADA

Arctic fox

Beaufort Sea

Pine forest

Polar bears

Arctic Ocean

Laptev Sea

Reindeer

Hudson Bay

Queen Elizabeth Islands

Ellesmere Island

NORTH POLE
✴

RUSSIA

Ice-breaker

Baffin Island

Huskies

SVALBARD (NORWAY)

GREENLAND (DENMARK)

Greenland Sea

Fishing

Arctic cod

NORWAY

42

Fishing

ICELAND

Spotted wolffish

ARCTIC CIRCLE

SWEDEN

FINLAND

0   1000km

0   500miles

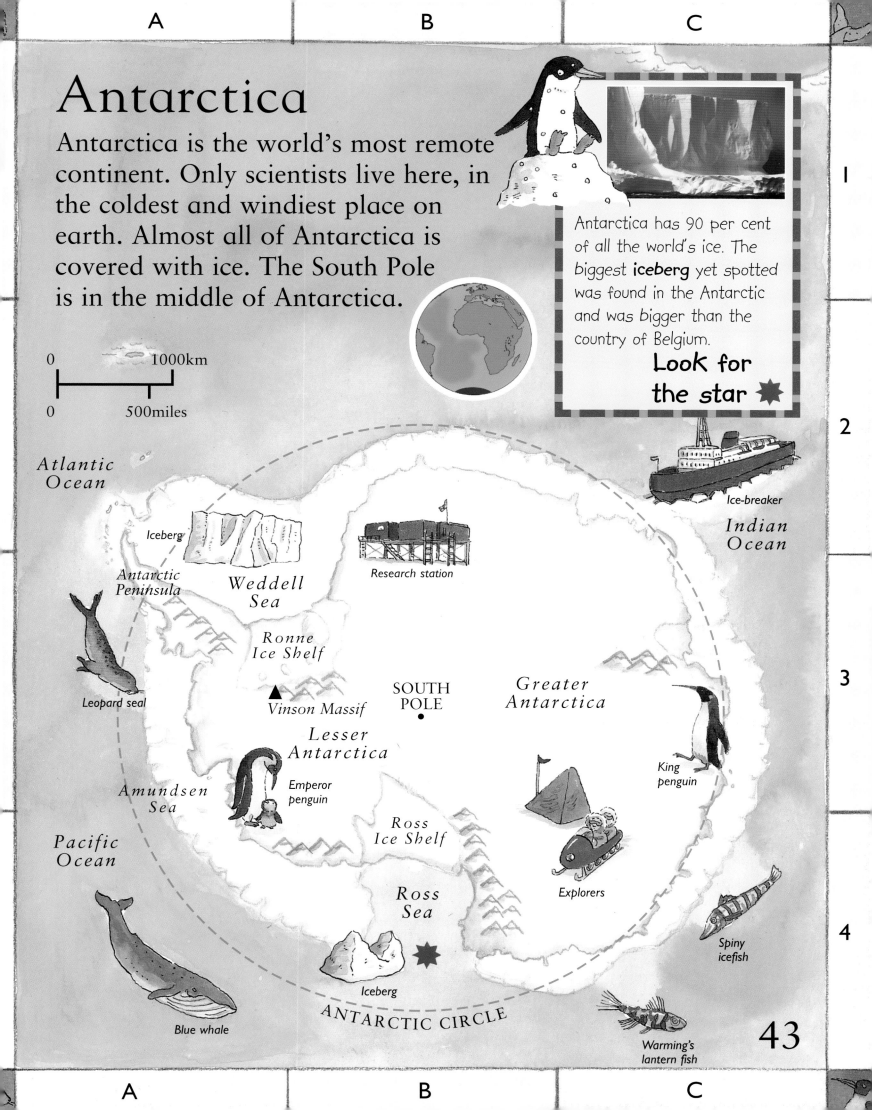

Antarctica

Antarctica is the world's most remote continent. Only scientists live here, in the coldest and windiest place on earth. Almost all of Antarctica is covered with ice. The South Pole is in the middle of Antarctica.

0   1000km

0   500miles

Antarctica has 90 per cent of all the world's ice. The biggest **iceberg** yet spotted was found in the Antarctic and was bigger than the country of Belgium.

Look for the star ✴

Atlantic Ocean

Iceberg

Antarctic Peninsula

Weddell Sea

Research station

Ice-breaker

Indian Ocean

Leopard seal

Ronne Ice Shelf

▲
Vinson Massif

SOUTH POLE
•

Greater Antarctica

King penguin

Lesser Antarctica

Emperor penguin

Amundsen Sea

Ross Ice Shelf

Explorers

Pacific Ocean

Ross Sea

✴

Spiny icefish

Iceberg

ANTARCTIC CIRCLE

Blue whale

Warming's lantern fish

43

1

ARCTIC CIRCLE

Fishing

Deep sea submersible

Car ferry

Blue whale

Cruise liner

2

TROPIC OF CANCER

Oil rig

Caribbean Sea

Scuba diving

Atlantic Ocean

Fishing

EQUATOR

Pacific Ocean

Freight ship

TROPIC OF CAPRICORN

3

Fishing

The oceans

Seen from space, the earth looks blue. This is because almost three quarters of the planet is covered with water. The earth has four great oceans, the Pacific, Atlantic, Indian and Arctic oceans. The Pacific is the biggest of these oceans.

Oil rig

Factory fishing ship

4

Iceberg

PRIME MERIDIAN

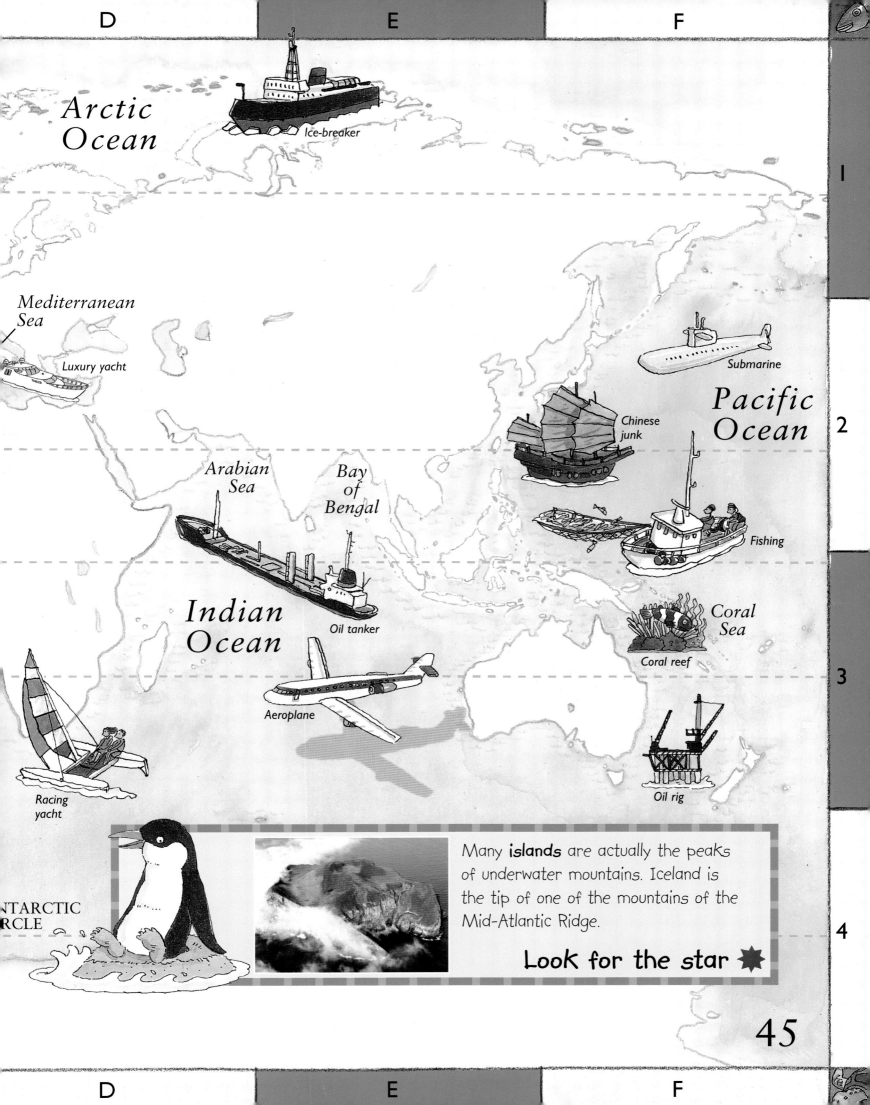

Arctic Ocean

Ice-breaker

Mediterranean Sea

Luxury yacht

Pacific Ocean

Submarine

Chinese junk

Fishing

Arabian Sea

Bay of Bengal

Indian Ocean

Oil tanker

Coral Sea

Coral reef

Aeroplane

Racing yacht

Oil rig

ANTARCTIC CIRCLE

Many **islands** are actually the peaks of underwater mountains. Iceland is the tip of one of the mountains of the Mid-Atlantic Ridge.

Look for the star ✦

Index